THE THE HARE, AND THE MARE

A story of kindness and bravery

Written by
Tiffany Hutorow

Illustrated by
Scott Hutorow &
Tiffany Hutorow

The Bear, the Hare, and the Mare
Copyright © 2023 Tiffany Hutorow
All rights reserved.
ISBN: 9798863067353

www.fecstable.com
Instagram: fecstable

The Bear, the Hare, and the Mare
Written by Tiffany Hutorow
Illustrated by Scott Hutorow
and Tiffany Hutorow
Edited by Sugandha Gupta
and Tammy Pollock

The art for this book was created with acrylic paint on primed canvas.

Summary: A caring hare finds herself on an adventure, helping a bear with no hair and a mare in despair. Will the hare find the bear some outerwear before winter?

To my *daughters* Mazie
and Aliza, who inspire me
to be better every day.

To my *mom*.

To my *nieces*.

There once was a bear.

His name was Pierre.

Pierre was a bear with no hair.

There once was a hare.

Her name was Claire.

Claire was a very *caring* hare.

Claire, the hare, smelt something in the air.

It was the smell of a bear.

She was surprised to see a bear with no hair.

She wondered how a bear would fare with nothing to wear.

The hare *cared* the bear had no hair.

Claire *dared* to approach the bear.

She said, "Hello, my name is Claire,
and you look like you are in despair."

The bear said, "Hello, my name is Pierre, and I am in despair.

Winter is coming, and I *need* something to wear."

Claire said to Pierre, "I can help you. I am aware of a rare mare.

She is a curly-haired mare.

I met this mare at an animal fair.

She has lots of hair, maybe she will *share*."

Pierre, the bear, and Claire, the hare, went to the animal fair.

Together they looked for the rare curly-haired mare.

The bear and the hare were an unusual *pair*.

They arrived at the fair where they saw a rare curly-haired stallion.

Pierre said to Claire, "I thought you said it was a rare curly-haired mare."

Claire hopped over to the stallion and said, "I swear there was a mare at this animal fair."

"You are *right*," the stallion told the hare.

"My name is Blaire, and I am worried about my sister, Flare.

I cannot find her anywhere.

We were playing a game called Dare when she left the fair to go to a scary, dark lair."

Claire said to Blaire, "Don't you worry, we will go to the dark lair and *find* Flare."

Pierre, the bear, Claire, the hare, and Blaire, the stallion, set out for the scary dark lair.

They were *searching* for Flare, the mare.

When they got close to the lair, Pierre said to Claire and Blaire, "Just so you are aware, this is the way to my den.

It's not a scary, dark lair, it's my *home*.

I have not seen a mare around there."

"We won't give up on Flare," said Claire.

They searched and searched but didn't see her anywhere.

Blaire said to Claire and Pierre,
"*Look* over there, it's Flare."

Flare called out to Blaire, "Beware,
my tail is caught in a bear snare."

Flare was in despair because her tail was caught in a snare.

Blaire was worried for his sister, Flare.

Pierre was in despair because he still had nothing to wear.

But, Claire *cared* about Blaire, Flare, and Pierre.

Claire hopped over to Flare and gnawed on the snare.

Flare was *free*, although she lost some curly hair in the snare.

"What can I do to repay you for setting me *free*?" Flare asked Claire.

Claire said, "If I could have some of the hair that came loose from the snare, I'd give it to my *friend* Pierre."

Flare said, "Of course, I'd *love* to *share*."

Blaire then said to Claire, "Is there anything I can do to repay you for *saving* my sister, Flare." Claire said, "Can you spare some of your curly hair for my friend Pierre?"

Blaire responded, "Of course, I'd *love* to *share* some of my curly hair."

Claire gathered the hair and they *all* returned to the animal fair.

Claire then prepared the hair, laid it in a square, and knit some outerwear.

"It's perfect, Claire! Is there anything I can do to repay you for making me some outerwear?" asked Pierre.

Claire said, "Not at all silly bear, you are my *friend* and I'm glad to see you are no longer in despair."

Pierre declared, in the wide, open air, "I've never met anyone as *caring, daring,* and *brave* as you, Claire.

I will make it my mission to help others because you have inspired me to be a *better* bear."

And off they went on a mission to *help* those in despair.

Nothing could compare to the *caring* bear and hare.

They were indeed an *extraordinary pair*.

*F*un Facts

- Curly-haired horses are unique because they are the only hypoallergenic horse breed. This means, they are less likely to cause an allergic reaction. Their breed is called Bashkir Curly and their hair, mane, and tail can be curly or wavy.

- A female adult horse is called a mare and a male adult horse is called a stallion.

- Hares are different from bunnies. Hares are wild and have longer ears and longer legs. Their hearing is exceptional, and they run faster too.

- Black bears can climb trees, swim in lakes and rivers, and have excellent sight and smell. During winters, they hibernate. This is where bears are in a dormant state for months. They are in their dens, and they don't need to eat or drink.

Nature is full of interesting plants and animals. We can be *kind, caring,* and *brave* like Claire and Pierre by helping others and taking care of the environment for creatures like bears, hares, and wild horses.

Acknowledgements

My daughters who inspired me to write a children's book and rhymed with me during the development of the book.

My kind and supportive husband who illustrated all the hares and the bear on the first page of the book.

My kindhearted stepmom, Tammy, who continuously helped edit the book.

My dad who showed me there is no limit to what we can accomplish and to always follow your dreams.

My mom, who always encouraged me. Her teachings emphasized the significance of trying my best, regardless of failure. She has motivated me to make the most out of the time I've been given.

All the supportive family and friends I am blessed to have in my life.

About the Author

Tiffany strives to make a difference through her writing and enjoys educating readers. Tiffany's debut children's book, "The Bear, the Hare, and the Mare," is a heartwarming story. It encourages readers to be kind, brave, and compassionate.

The book started when Tiffany and her daughters, aged 4 and 6, were rhyming while doing errands. By the time they finished their errands, the story was nearly complete. The illustrations began one weekend morning, while Tiffany and her daughters were painting, and her husband, Scott, painted a hare. His contribution led to every hare being painted in the book and the bear on the first page. This book is truly a family collaboration.

Manufactured by Amazon.ca
Acheson, AB